Spotlight on the
MAYA, AZTEC, and INCA CIVILIZATIONS

Ancient INCA GOVERNMENT

Amy Hayes

PowerKiDS press.

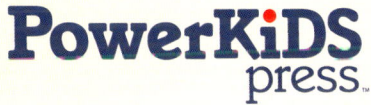

New York

Published in 2017 by The Rosen Publishing Group, Inc.
29 East 21st Street, New York, NY 10010

Copyright © 2017 by The Rosen Publishing Group, Inc.

All rights reserved. No part of this book may be reproduced in any form without permission in writing from the publisher, except by a reviewer.

Editor: Sarah Machajewski

Photo Credits: Cover (foreground) Neale Cousland/Shutterstock.com; cover (background) shipfactory/Shutterstock.com; p. 4 https://commons.wikimedia.org/wiki/File:Inca_Empire.svg; p. 5 Anton_Ivanov/Shutterstock.com; p. 7 https://commons.wikimedia.org/wiki/File:Manco_Capac_Statue_Lima_La_Victoria.jpg; p. 8 Adwo/Shutterstock.com; p. 9 Matyas Rehak/Shutterstock.com; p. 10 https://commons.wikimedia.org/wiki/File:Waskhar_lifetime_portrait.jpg; p. 11 Illustration of Huascar Inca from 'Historia y Genealogia Real de los Reyes Incas del Peru, de sus hechos, costumbres, trajes y manera de Gobierno', known as the Codice Murua (vellum), Spanish School, (16th century)/Private Collection/Bridgeman Images; p. 12 Science & Society Picture Library/SSPL/Getty Images; p. 13 DEA PICTURE LIBRARY/De Agostini Picture Library/Getty Images; p. 14 Inca Storehouses (woodcut), Poma de Ayala, Felipe Huaman (1526-1613)/Private Collection/Bridgeman Images; p. 15 https://commons.wikimedia.org/wiki/File:Ollantaytambo_granaries_Stevage.jpg; p. 17 Lynn Johnson/National Geographic/Getty Images; p. 18 De Agostini/G. Dagli Orti/De Agostini Picture Library/Getty Images; p. 19 Peruvian warriors of the Inca period/Universal History Archive/UIG / Bridgeman Images; p. 20 Jess Kraft/Shutterstock.com; p. 21 sunsinger/Shutterstock.com; p. 22 Marco Maccarini/Stockbyte/Getty Images; pp. 23, 27 DEA / G. DAGLI ORTI/De Agostini Picture Library/Getty Images; p. 25 Agne Alminaite/Shutterstock.com; p. 29 Werner Forman/Universal Images Group/Getty Images.

Library of Congress Cataloging-in-Publication Data

Names: Hayes, Amy, author.
Title: Ancient Inca government / Amy Hayes.
Description: New York : PowerKids Press, [2016] | Series: Spotlight on the
  Maya, Aztec, and Inca civilizations | Includes index.
Identifiers: LCCN 2016002137 | ISBN 9781499419481 (pbk.) | ISBN 9781499419511 (library bound) | ISBN 9781499419498 (6 pack)
Subjects: LCSH: Incas--Politics and government--Juvenile literature.
Classification: LCC F3429.3.P65 H36 2016 | DDC 985/.01--dc23
LC record available at http://lccn.loc.gov/2016002137

CPSIA Compliance Information: Batch #BS16PK: For further information contact Rosen Publishing, New York, New York at 1-800-237-9932.

CONTENTS

An Inca Morning 4
What Kind of Government? 6
Sapa Inca, Son of Inti 8
Sapa Inca, Ruler of All 10
The Four *Suyus* 12
A Pyramid of Organization 14
Ayllus and Towns 16
Military Strength 18
Conquered People 20
Laws and Punishment 22
Taxes and the *Mit'a* 24
A Government-Run Economy 26
Careful Record Keeping 28
The Inca World 30
Glossary 31
Index 32
Primary Source List 32
Websites 32

AN INCA MORNING

The bright dawn hits the slopes of the Andes Mountains. To the east, the brilliant greens of the Amazon basin hide the many birds whose calls welcome a new day. Soon, morning will spread across the Andes, reaching the western coast that faces the Pacific Ocean. The Inca Empire begins to wake up.

A child gets up and wraps a cloth of alpaca wool around her body, pinning it in place. She walks outside. The farmland she lives on is a large, flat step near the top of a steep mountain. She looks up into the sky and glances at the bright disk that has brought the dawn. It is Inti, the Inca sun god.

The child thinks of the Sapa Inca, the emperor of the Incas. The Inca government has determined everything—where she lives, what she wears, and what crops her family grows.

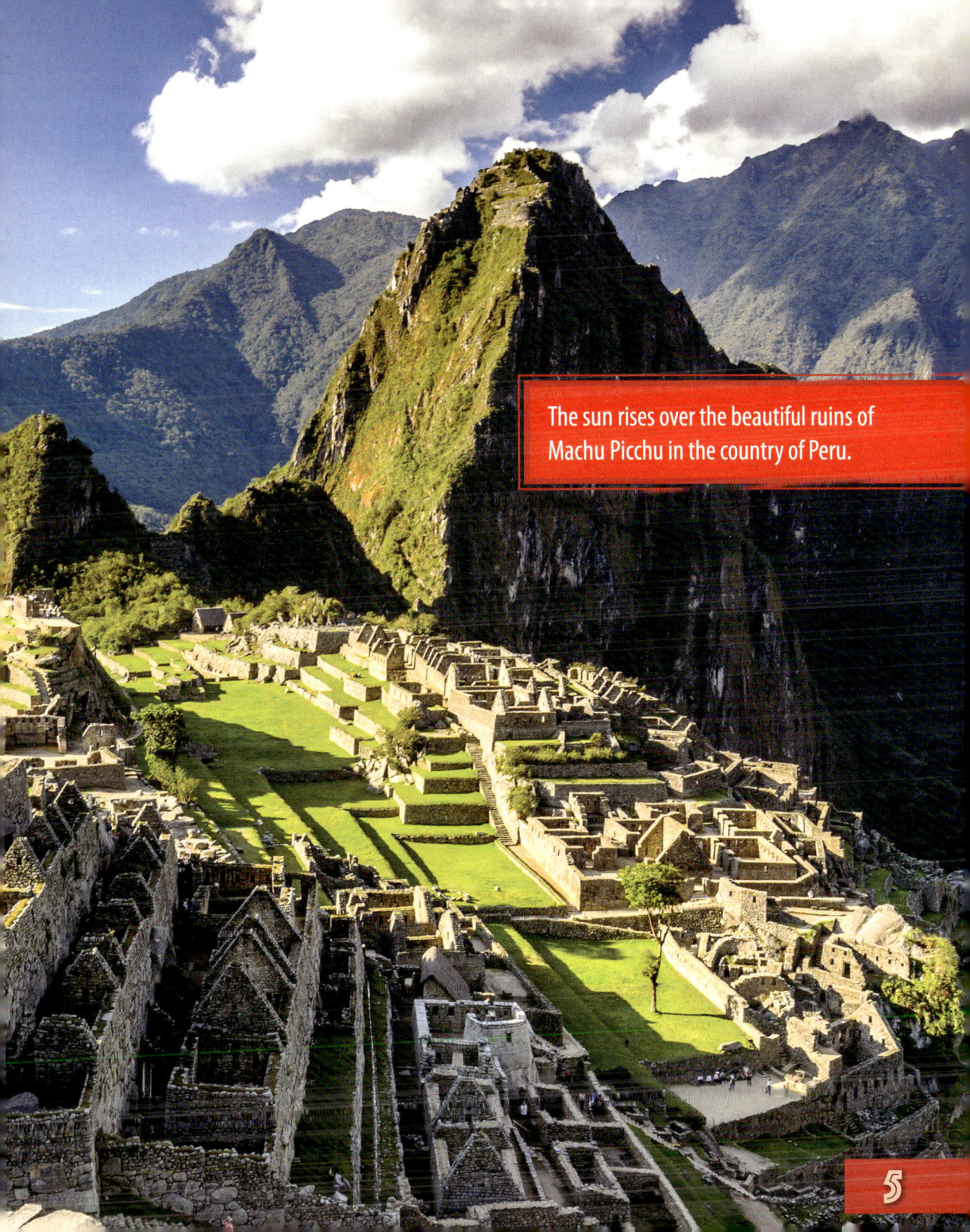

The sun rises over the beautiful ruins of Machu Picchu in the country of Peru.

WHAT KIND OF GOVERNMENT?

The Inca government was a big part of the lives of people who lived in the **Sacred** Valley and beyond. It determined how people spent their days. All people in Inca society had a certain job to do, whether they were farmers and laborers or the emperor and his government officials.

It isn't easy to put the Inca government in a category. The Sapa Inca ruled everything. Some people would call this a **dictatorship**, because one man was in charge of the entire government. However, it's not that simple.

In many ways the Inca government was also like an oligarchy. In an oligarchy, a small group of people have the most power, while most people have little power. The Sapa Inca had several high-powered advisors who helped him rule the common people.

Finally, some parts of the Inca government worked on the people's behalf. Many committees decided things as a group. This is sort of like a republic, where representatives come together to make decisions for groups of citizens. However, the committee members weren't elected as representatives in republics are.

The first Sapa Inca was Manco Capac. Every powerful family of the Inca government descended from him.

SAPA INCA, SON OF INTI

The role of the Sapa Inca was both spiritual and political. He was said to be the son of Inti, the god of the sun. Because of this, all of the Sapa Inca's rulings were considered **divine**. His decisions and actions were said to be what the gods wanted.

This so-called Gate of the Sun stands in present-day Bolivia. Created by a pre-Inca civilization, it may have been a kind of calendar. It features a carving of an important god.

The dark stone on the lower half of this building is all that remains of Coricancha. Built sometime in the 15th century, it was the most sacred place in the Inca Empire. The Spanish Church of Santo Domingo was later built above it.

A Sapa Inca had many religious duties while running the Inca Empire. As the human representative of the sun god, he performed **rituals** that symbolized the changing of the seasons. For example, he was the first to break ground at the plowing festival. He led the harvest offerings to the sun god. During the first day of the Sun Festival, the Sapa Inca alone saw the sun rise and strike the golden wall of Coricancha, the Temple of the Sun.

SAPA INCA, RULER OF ALL

The Sapa Inca was very powerful in terms of his political duties. He commanded the military, met with his advisors, settled disputes, and took charge of his family group. Traveling from city to city, he would give speeches from atop a stepped stone platform in a public plaza.

Beyond these public appearances, the Sapa Inca was very **secluded**. It was believed that the touch of a Sapa Inca would carry a blessing. However, if the emperor looked upon a citizen who was unworthy of his gaze, his glance would kill them. Because of this, he often sat behind a screen.

Those who did meet the Sapa Inca had to follow very strict rules. People had to take their shoes off and bow. They had to carry a heavy load on their back the entire time they spoke to the Sapa Inca, just to show respect.

Huáscar Inca, emperor of the Inca, was born around 1502 and lived until about 1532. He was one of the last Sapa Incas.

The Sapa Inca was transported on a litter, which is a seat carried on men's shoulders.

THE FOUR *SUYUS*

The great expanse of the Inca Empire was broken up into four parts, which were called *suyus*. These were the Chinchaysuyu, Antisuyu, Collasuyu, and Contisuyu. The whole of the Inca Empire was called Tawantinsuyu, which in the Quechua language means "four parts together." The Chinchaysuyu was in the Northwest. The Antisuyu was in the Northeast. They made up the upper half of the empire. The Collasuyu ran to the South, and the Contisuyu was a smaller territory to the Southwest. They formed the lower half of the empire.

Cuzco, the great capital city, was located in the Sacred Valley. It was in the center of the empire. From Cuzco, four roads led to the *suyus*. Average citizens weren't allowed to use these roads. They were specifically for messengers, government projects, and the military.

QUIPU

A powerful leader called an *apo* led each of the four *suyus*. Apos were almost like emperors in their own right and acted as important advisors to the Sapa Inca.

This is a woodcut of an Inca citizen holding a quipu, which was a record-keeping tool. People like him worked for the Inca government.

A PYRAMID OF ORGANIZATION

Apos ruled regions that were generally organized by **ethnic** group. The Inca Empire was incredibly large and expanded regularly. Organization was essential as the empire continued to grow.

The Inca Empire was organized in a very mathematical way. It depended on the population. The empire had about 80 provinces. Provinces were groups of about 20,000 households. Each province had a governor who reported to the *apo*. Under each governor, there were officials called curacas who each looked after 10,000 households. These officials

This woodcut shows a man with a quipu, as well as Inca storehouses. He is probably recording what's being stored inside.

> Curacas and *camayocs* were in charge of making sure taxes were taken, labor requirements were met, and that storehouses, or *qollqa*, were full.

QOLLQA AT OLLANTAYTAMBO, PERU

had curacas under them who each were responsible for 5,000 households. Then, these each had curacas under them who looked after 1,000 households. This continued all the way down until there was a person called a *camayoc* who looked after 10 households. Some historians estimate that for every 10,000 workers, there were 1,300 government officials.

AYLLUS AND TOWNS

Inca society was organized into communities called ayllus. Ayllus were networks of family groups that lived in the same area. People of the Andean region lived in ayllus long before the Inca came to power, but the Inca government transformed them into centers of productivity.

Ayllus were made of about 10 to 20 different families. Each ayllu was expected to be **self-sufficient**, so it had to grow all the food it needed on its own. All members of the ayllu who were capable of working had to farm the land they were given. The work was shared among the community rather than falling to just one person.

Married men had to leave the ayllu for a few weeks or months each year to perform a labor requirement for the government. When they left, other community members would step in to take over their work.

Today in Cuzco, Peru, women still **thresh** quinoa, which is a seed commonly grown in ayllus and eaten throughout the Inca Empire.

17

MILITARY STRENGTH

The Inca Empire expanded rapidly. The Inca's large army allowed the government to easily take over lands. The Inca army was large because all men were required to serve in the military for a period of time. After completing their service, they were allowed to return to their ayllu.

The army also grew when the Inca took soldiers from their enemies' armies after they were defeated. While many civilizations killed their enemies, the Inca spared enemy soldiers' lives. They killed only the army leaders.

In this woodcut, the Inca army is shown attacking the Spanish, who took over Cuzco in 1533.

18

> Inca warriors used weapons made of stone, wood, and bronze. They carried shields to protect the front and back of their body.

Although the Inca Empire had a huge army, many Inca soldiers weren't highly trained. Many times, battles weren't even fought. Instead, the Inca would send messengers to convince other groups to surrender to the Inca in exchange for land and goods. If they didn't agree, the Inca sent their huge army to the city. After seeing the size of the force, enemy leaders generally surrendered.

CONQUERED PEOPLE

The Inca Empire's strong military force took over nearly 100 different groups of people who lived in the Andes Mountains. In a short period of time, there were more people the Incas had conquered in the empire than Incas themselves. The Incas had several ways of dealing with this. For example, those who hadn't resisted the Inca and joined the empire were given special privileges and gifts.

TARMA, PERU

> To this day, people farm high into the Andes, just as their ancestors did before them.

People who resisted the Inca were dealt with in a different way, through a policy called *mitima*. After the Inca military defeated them, the people were moved from their homelands and forced to resettle in areas where loyalty to the Inca was strong. As these people were kept away from their home, their motivation to fight against Inca rule faded.

The Inca government filled in the empty land with *mitmakonas*, who were people who showed loyalty to the Incas through their labor and by paying taxes. The *mitmakonas* were supposed to set a good example for the people in the areas that rebelled. It was a great honor to be chosen as a *mitmakona*.

LAWS AND PUNISHMENT

Every government has laws that people must follow. Each government also has its own way of dealing with people who break those laws. Inca law enforcement was very strict, but fairer than many civilizations throughout history. In general, curacas, *camayocs*, and other local officials were supposed to make sure people followed the law. If a law was broken, the person accused of the crime could defend themselves, and government officials considered their **testimony** carefully.

INCA ALTAR
ISLA DEL SOL, BOLIVIA

The punishments in the Inca society were **brutal**. Here, a soldier removes a nobleman's eye.

If a person was found guilty, they received harsh punishment. The Inca Empire didn't have prisons, so going to jail wasn't an option. Instead, physical pain was used as a way to convince others to follow the law. Stealing was punished by whipping. Worse crimes were dealt with by dropping large rocks on a person's back, other forms of torture, and death. As terrible as these punishments sound, they were rarely needed. There was little crime in the Inca Empire.

TAXES AND THE *MIT'A*

Inca society was highly dependent on taxes. Every person in the Inca Empire was expected to pay taxes, but not with money. In fact, the Incas didn't have any form of currency. Taxes were given in the form of the labor and goods people produced.

Farmers were expected to contribute food from their crops. Each ayllu was expected to contribute two-thirds of its total crops as a tax. Half of this was placed in a *qollqa* for military troops and for use in times of **famine**. The other half was distributed to priests to use as **sacrifices** to the gods and in religious celebrations.

There was also a form of tax called the *mit'a*. The *mit'a* was a labor requirement adult male citizens had to perform. Citizens left the ayllu from a few weeks to a few months to work as soldiers, farmers, miners, builders, and more. Women worked at home by **weaving** or caring for children. The *mit'a* gave the Inca Empire beautiful buildings and temples, food, bridges, roads, and a large army. Through their work, each citizen played a part in making the society strong.

When a man and wife married, the man became a *puric*, which is a Quechua word for "taxpayer." Each time the family had a child, the Inca government gave them more farmland, shown here. This provided more land to feed their family, but also made them responsible for more taxes.

A GOVERNMENT-RUN ECONOMY

The Inca government completely controlled the society's economy. This meant there was little chance for social mobility, as citizens couldn't make a living by owning stores or businesses. However, the centrally planned economy benefitted the people in many ways.

For one, every person was given the resources they needed to live—land and housing were provided, as was food when famine struck. No one was homeless or starved to death in the Inca Empire. Everyone, from the young to the old, was expected to pull their own weight. If a person was too sick or old to work in the fields, they were taken care of by the government.

Once the Inca were growing enough food to feed the empire, a whole class of artisans appeared. Instead of worrying about having enough food to eat, people spent time perfecting their skills at pottery, metalwork, and weaving. Beautifully woven cloth was a treasure in Inca society.

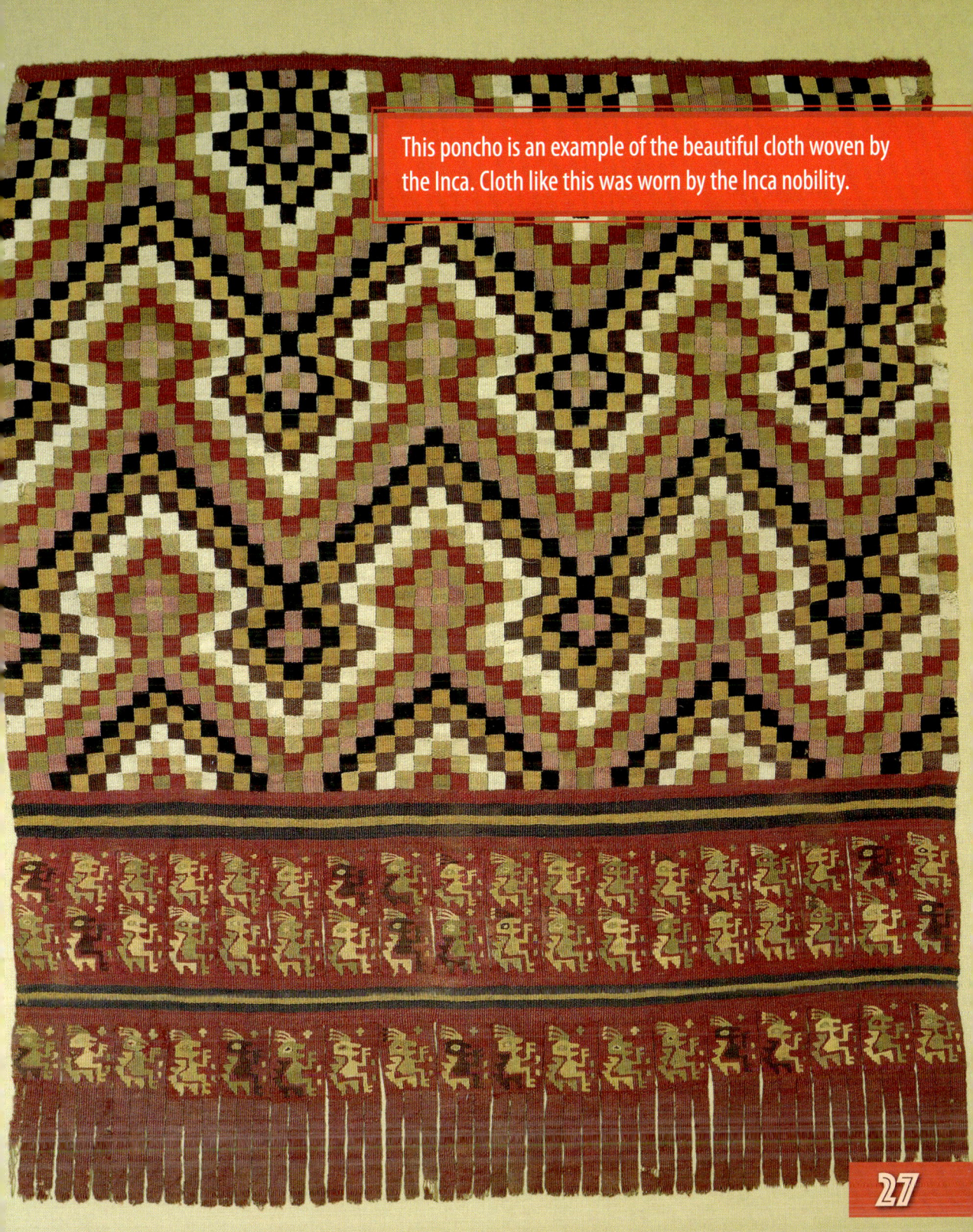

This poncho is an example of the beautiful cloth woven by the Inca. Cloth like this was worn by the Inca nobility.

CAREFUL RECORD KEEPING

With a huge army, an expanding empire, many advisors, and a government centered on one man, it may seem as though the Inca Empire was hard to manage. How did curacas make sure enough food was stored in case of famine? How did the Sapa Inca know when goods from one *suyu* would make it to another? How did *apos* decide how many workers to send to a gold mine? The key to running the empire was all in the record keeping.

Record keepers were called *quipucamayocs*. It was their job to keep records of everything happening in their province, much like a modern-day accountant.

The Inca spoke a family of related languages called Quechua, but they did not have a writing system. Instead, *quipucamayocs* used a **complex** device of knotted strings called a quipu to record taxes, animal herds, goods produced, *mit'a* requirements, people, and other aspects of life.

> Quipus were extremely important to the Inca. Sometimes, more than one record keeper kept track of the activity in the ayllu. His quipu were used as backup in case the first was lost or damaged.

THE INCA WORLD

The Inca government is sometimes difficult to sort out. The government controlled the economy, but the system was designed to benefit the people. Through regulating the goods produced and the services performed through the *mit'a*, the society offered a lot to its citizens. There was a strict class structure and the Sapa Inca held complete power, but the goal of the government was to care for every citizen. Common people had little say in their government. Yet, crime was low, famine was rare, and homelessness didn't exist.

As experts discover more about Inca society, the culture grows more impressive. The remains of the Inca civilization remind the world that the Inca had a complex and **unique** way of life. It is important to think about the lessons we can learn from this ancient society and the government that controlled it.

GLOSSARY

brutal (BROO-tuhl): Extremely violent or harsh.

complex (kahm-PLEHKS): Having a number of parts. Also, sometimes difficult to understand.

dictatorship (dihk-TAY-tohr-ship): A government run by one person who has complete power.

divine (dih-VYN): Of, from, or like a god or gods.

ethnic (ETH-nik): Having to do with people who share a common national or cultural background.

famine (FAA-muhn): An extreme lack of food.

ritual (RIH-choo-uhl): A religious ceremony.

sacred (SAY-kruhd): Regarded with great respect because of its religious importance or connection with the divine.

sacrifice (SAA-kruh-fyce): Someone or something that is offered to a god or ruler. Also, the offering of someone or something in this fashion.

seclude (sih-KLOOD): To keep away from other people.

self-sufficient (SELF–suh-FIH-shunt): Needing no outside help.

testimony (TEHS-tih-moh-nee): A formal statement, especially concerning a crime or in a court of law.

thresh (THRESH): To separate grain from a plant.

unique (yoo-NEEK): Special or different.

weaving (WEE-ving): The art of making cloth by crossing strands of thread or yarn over and over.

INDEX

A
Amazon basin, 4
Andes Mountains, 4, 20, 21
Antisuyu, 12
apos, 12, 14, 28
ayllu, 16, 18, 24, 28

C
camayocs, 15, 22
Chinchaysuyu, 12
Church of Santo Domingo, 9
Collasuyu, 12
Contisuyu, 12
Coricancha, 9
curacas, 14, 15, 22, 28
Cuzco, 12, 16, 18

H
Huáscar Inca, 10

I
Inti, 4, 8

M
Machu Picchu, 5
Manco Capac, 7
mit'a, 24, 28, 30
mitima, 21
mitmakona, 21

P
Pacific Ocean, 4
Peru, 5, 15, 16, 20

Q
qollqa, 15, 24
quipu, 12, 13, 14, 28
quipucamayoc, 28

S
Sacred Valley, 6, 12
Sapa Inca, 4, 6, 7, 8, 9, 10, 11, 12, 28, 30
Spanish, 9, 18

T
Tawantinsuyu, 12

PRIMARY SOURCE LIST

Page 5: Machu Picchu. Built by the Inca. Stone and earth. 16th century. Located in the Andes Mountains, Peru.

Page 8: Gate of the Sun. Built by the Tiwanaku people. Andesite. ca. 400 and 900. Located in the Province of Ingavi, Bolivia.

Page 13: Inca man holding a quipu. Created by Felipe Guaman Poma de Ayala. Published in *The First New Chronicle and Good Government*. Engraving. 1612–1615. Now kept in The Royal Library, Copenhagen, Denmark.

Page 18: Inca army attacking the Spanish. Created by Felipe Guaman Poma de Ayala. Published in *The First New Chronicle and Good Government*. Engraving. 1612–1615. Now kept in The Royal Library, Copenhagen, Denmark.

WEBSITES

Due to the changing nature of Internet links, PowerKids Press has developed an online list of websites related to the subject of this book. This site is updated regularly. Please use this link to access the list: www.powerkidslinks.com/soac/incg